MW01286954

"This republic: represents a timely and most welcome reminder that questions about the proper role of creedal statements, the relationship between biblical exegesis and systematic theology, and the degree of continuity between evangelicalism and the past are perennial, important, and worthy of our careful attention."

Matthew C. Bingham,
Lecturer in Systematic Theology and Church History,
Oak Hill College

"Here we have a distillation of choice theological wisdom from one of the greatest pastor-theologians of all time. John Gill was a faithful minister of the same Baptist church for more than fifty years as well as a masterful theologian of the Great Tradition. In this attractive new edition, the great Gill speaks again to the Lord's people in our own time."

Timothy George,
Distinguished Professor at Beeson Divinity School
of Samford University; General Editor,
Reformation Commentary on Scripture (29 vols.)

"I know of few people in the history of the church better qualified to speak to the issue 'what is theology?' than John Gill, the 18th century English Baptist theologian. Having written a commentary on every book of the Bible, and having engaged every relevant theological issue of the 18th century in polemical tracts, and having worked through a massive number of the early church fathers in discussing the doctrines of grace in church history, he made the writing of a systematic theology one of the last things that he did. He was well prepared exegetically, historically, and polemically to engage the issue. This introductory volume to a series of the works of Gill is important for every person who values the revelation that God has given us in holy scripture."

Tom J. Nettles,
Senior Professor of Historical Theology,
The Southern Baptist Theological Seminary

"John Gill stood like a seawall against the flood of false doctrine eroding the foundations of the church in the eighteenth century. He fought for the truth because, like Athanasius, he knew that the practical Christian life grew out 'evangelical doctrine, spiritually understood, affectionately embraced, and powerfully and feelingly experienced.' This book, Gill's introduction to his massive *Body of Divinity*, lays down basic principles for deriving theology from the Bible and traces the development of theology from Adam to our present day."

Joel R. Beeke,
President, Puritan Reformed Theological Seminary

WHAT

is

THEOLOGY?

JOHN GILL

H&E
Publishing

What is theology?
© 2022 by H&E Publishing

Series: John Gill on the spiritual life
Series Editor: Christopher Ellis Osterbrock

Published by: H&E Publishing,
West Lorne, Ontario, Canada
www.hesedandemet.com

Source in Public Domain: John Gill, *A Body of
Doctrinal Divinity; or, A System of Evangelical Truths,
Deduced from the Sacred Scriptures. In Two Volumes,
Volume I* (London, 1769), 1–26.

Cover and layout design by Dustin Benge

Paperback ISBN: 978-1-77484-094-8
Ebook ISBN: 978-1-77484-095-5

THE *John Gill* PROJECT

In partnership with
The Andrew Fuller Center for Baptist Studies
& The London Lyceum

John Gill on the spiritual life

"*Let us therefore search the Scriptures, to see whether our doctrines are advanced according to them or not. Such a practice, I fear, is too little attended.*"

JOHN GILL

CONTENTS

SERIES PREFACE

These six little volumes which make up the series John Gill on the spiritual life are designed with both the scholar and local church in mind. Each volume is transcribed from Gill's *A Body of Doctrinal and Practical Divinity* (1769–1770), and yet edited in such a way as to enable Gill's vocabulary, formatting(headings, subheadings, etc.), and syntax be read with ease by the 21st-century reader. Full names and dates of historical figures are also added at first use to bring greater clarity to the data. Included in each volume are discussion questions for the purpose of small groups or personal edification. Though five of these volumes particularly focus on the spiritual formation of believers, *What is theology?* is an essential for developing a doctrinally rich inner life—as Gill would surely agree.

It is the endeavor of the John Gill Project to draw upon the rich spirituality at work in men like Gill, take it up fresh, and share it for the sake of godliness in our own churches today. May these sources be proven to magnify Christ and stir affections within his church.

Christopher Ellis Osterbrock

Series Editor

INTRODUCTION

The life and ministry of John Gill

"The Rev. Dr. John Gill was certainly one of the greatest and best of men."[1] Despite this superlative commendation, it is likely that you may have never heard of John Gill (1697–1771). Regrettably, Gill's name is unrecognizable among most Baptists. Historians certainly continue to discuss his life and thinking, but their numbers are small. As an historical figure, Gill remains in obscurity. This was not the case in his own day nor after his death, when his published writings were widely read and distributed in England and across the Atlantic to North America. One historian observes that "Gill was the natural theological leader of his

---

1   John Rippon, *A Brief Memoir of the Life and Writings of the Late Rev. John Gill, D. D.* (1838 repr. Harrisonburg, VA: Sprinkle Publications, 2006), 1.

day, for he had written more, published more, and defended more openly than any of his brethren ... He thus became the spokesman for Calvinist Dissent in general and for Baptists in particular."[2]

To rectify the lack of recognition of this towering figure in Baptist life, this modest biographical sketch seeks to introduce John Gill to new and inquiring audiences and thereby make him more well known. While Gill was an imperfect man, he is nevertheless worth remembering—and in several respects worth emulating. The facts of his life are by any standard extraordinary, Gill being a man of rare giftedness, industry, and constancy.

Childhood and education

John Gill was born on November 23, 1697, in Kettering, Northamptonshire. His parents Edward and Elizabeth raised him in a church of dissenters (non-Anglican Protestants in England). But in time they left to form a specifically Baptist congregation under the pastoral leadership of William Wallis (d. 1711), who had served as a teacher within

2   Olin C. Robison, "Legacy of John Gill," *The Baptist Quarterly* 24, no. 3 (July 1971): 113.

their dissenting congregation.

Gill excelled in academics as a child, demonstrating unusual diligence and intellectual capability. By the age of twelve he had mastered Latin and attained proficiency in Greek that garnered him praise from pastors with whom he interacted at the local bookstore. The young Gill was so often at the local bookstore, devouring all the learning he could, that those who wanted to assert the surety of a fact would say that it is as sure "as John Gill is in the bookseller's shop."[3]

Despite Gill's prodigious learning as a child, his formal education abruptly concluded before the age of twelve when the local school master decided to take his students to the daily prayer services of the Church of England. Maintaining their fervent dissenting convictions, Gill's parents removed him from the school. And yet, despite numerous efforts to provide Gill with a formal education, he ended up working with his father part-time in the woolen trade until he was about nineteen years old.

Gill's removal from school did little to curb his

3   Rippon, *Memoir*, 4.

educational progress. He continued to master the classical curriculum by improving his facility in Greek and Latin and by studying logic, rhetoric, and philosophy. During this time Gill devoted himself to learning Hebrew and reading the Protestant scholastic authors, both of which became defining features of his writings. Gill's self-taught knowledge of Hebrew was a contributing factor to his reception of an honorary doctorate from Marischal College, Aberdeen University. Likewise, his study of the Protestant scholastic authors left an indelible mark on his approach to theology.

Conversion, ministry, and family

Around the age of twelve, Gill was converted while hearing William Wallis preach from Genesis 3:9. While Gill had previously experienced transient conviction of sin and fear of judgment, he had now come to experience his definite need of and reliance on Christ's righteousness. Shortly after this experience Wallis died and was succeeded in the pastorate by his son, Thomas Wallis (d.1726). It was Thomas Wallis who baptized Gill in a nearby river after Gill publicly professed his faith in Christ on November 1, 1716, at the age of nineteen.

Gill became a member of the church on the following Sunday, participated in the Lord's Supper, and, unexpectedly, preached his first sermon from Isaiah 53. This sermon, given during a prayer meeting, was received well and he was asked back the following week. Gill's second sermon at the prayer meeting was preached on 1 Corinthians 2:2.

The Kettering congregation very quickly discerned Gill's ministerial gifts, and with the recommendation of his friends, he soon moved to Higham Ferrers to assist pastor John Davis' newly-planted church. Gill had hoped that Davis would guide him in his studies, but that aspiration went unfulfilled. What may have seemed a disappointment soon turned into a blessing, since during his ministry in Higham Ferrers Gill met his wife-to-be, Elizabeth Negus.

John and Elizabeth were married in 1718 and stayed faithful in marriage until her death in October, 1764. By all available accounts they enjoyed an exemplary Christian marriage as both John and Elizabeth loved and served one another. While Elizabeth diligently worked to allow Gill fruitful hours of study and ministry, Gill served Elizabeth through years of "appalling health, caused by difficult pregnancies, miscarriages, still-births, and sickly infants."[4]

John and Elizabeth had numerous children together, although only three survived past infancy. And of these three, only two survived into adulthood. Their daughter Elizabeth died at the age of thirteen in 1738. In a demonstration of fortitude, Gill preached the sermon for both his deceased daughter and wife at their respective funeral services.

A call to London

It was not long after marrying Elizabeth that Gill returned to Kettering to assist his home church. His time back in Kettering, while short-lived, saw much fruitful ministry. Soon after arriving back in Kettering, Gill was invited to preach for a church at Horselydown in Southwark that had recently lost its pastor, Benjamin Stinton (1677–1719). Stinton was the son-in-law of the church's founder, Benjamin Keach (1640–1704), who had been influential

---

4   Sharon James, "'The Weaker Vessel': John Gill's Reflections on Women, Marriage and Divorce," in *The Life and Thought of John Gill (1697–1771): A Tercentennial Appreciation*, ed. Michael A. G. Haykin, Studies in the History of Christian Thought 77 (Leiden: Brill, 1997), 216.

amongst Particular Baptists. After his initial invitation, Gill came back to preach multiple times and it was determined that he should be considered to fill the pastoral vacancy.

A large majority of the church voted to elect Gill as pastor on November 13, 1719, but some opposed his election, including the church's deacons. Regardless of the opposition, Gill accepted the call to become their next pastor the following Sunday. Controversy erupted with the upshot that Gill's supporters separated from the other members while maintaining their identity as the congregation started by Keach. Gill was finally ordained as their pastor on March 20 of the following year.

Gill's conviction of his call to the church at Horselydown factored into his early success in London. As B.R. White wrote of Gill's tumultuous call to the church:

> For Gill's own stand was the key to the situation: if he remained firm long enough he could hope to live down the initial opposition; if he faltered, his own future as a minister in London was in grave doubt. Whilst there can be no doubt that his firmness stemmed from his own certainty that this was God's

will for him the prospect was one before which most
men of his age would have quailed.[5]

His steadfastness in the face of opposition set the tone for
his ministry and was a sign of things to come for Gill as a
pastor-theologian.

Ministry in London

As Gill began his first full-time ministry, his preaching
was met with great success. Early on the church found it
difficult to accommodate all who wanted to hear the young
preacher, even with their spacious accommodations.

Gill's preaching also led to his first publication in 1724,
a funeral sermon for one of the church's deacons. It was
also in this year that Gill began to preach sermons from the
Song of Solomon that eventually became the basis for one
of his most well-known works, *An Exposition of the Book of
Solomon's Song*, published first in 1728. The book's republication in three editions during his life, as well as its posthu-
mous republication, evince its popularity. Gill's memoirist

5   B.R. White, "John Gill in London (1719–1729): A Biographical Fragment,"
     The Baptist Quarterly 22 (1967–1968): 75.

notes that "the publication of this Exposition served very much to make Mr. Gill known."[6] The renowned preacher C.H. Spurgeon—who later pastored the same congregation in London—commented of this work that it was "The best thing Gill ever did ... Those who despise it have never read it, or are incapable of elevated spiritual feelings."[7]

Gill the controversialist

Early on Gill also established himself as a controversialist, or polemical writer. The first of such pieces centered on the doctrine of baptism. While Gill became conversant with the history of the church and drank especially deeply from the wells of the Reformed scholastic writers, he nevertheless maintained staunch Baptist convictions until his death. So when Gill penned one of his forays into controversial print in 1726, he wrote a defense of believer's baptism in response to Matthias Maurice (1684–1738), who pastored an Independent church in Northamptonshire. Gill's two

6   Rippon, *Memoir*, 24.
7   C H. Spurgeon, "Commenting and Commentaries: Two Lectures Addressed to the Students of The Pastor's College, Metropolitan Tabernacle, Together with A Catalogue of Biblical Commentaries and Expositions," in *Lectures to My Students: Four Volumes in One* (Pasadena: Pilgrim Publications, 1990), 113.

works written in response to Maurice furthered his reputation, not only among Baptists in England, but also in North America.

Many, if not most, of Gill's writings were occasioned by the spread of some doctrine or idea he believed was injurious to the gospel. Gill published his *Exposition of the Book of Solomon's Song* at the behest of his church, but Gill's main aim in publishing it was to defend the book's authority and canonicity in light of recent challenges. The same year, Gill published *The Prophecies of the Old Testament, Respecting the Messiah, Considered and Proved to Be Literally Fulfilled in Jesus* to demonstrate the fulfillment of messianic prophecies in Jesus through a literal interpretation of Scripture.

Gill willingly engaged in controversy for the sake of what he believed was true, even at the risk of personal cost. In a debate with Abraham Taylor (fl. 1726–1740) over the doctrine of justification, he was cautioned against furthering their disagreement. He was told that continued debate could result in a loss of reputation and income if he lost the support of some wealthy subscribers to his books. Nevertheless, Gill is reported to have responded, "Don't tell me of losing ... I value nothing, in comparison of Gospel truths. I am not afraid to be poor."[8]

Gill not only resisted careerist tendencies, but he unrelentingly prosecuted his arguments. John Wesley, with whom Gill controverted, said that "he is a positive man, and fights for his own opinions through thick and thin." Augustus Toplady (1740–1778) held Gill's argumentative efforts in high regard when he wrote the following complimentary comparison: "I believe it may be said of my learned friend, as it was of the Duke of Marlborough, that he never fought a battle which he did not win."[9]

Gill the pastor-theologian

Within a decade of starting his ministry in London, Gill had earned sufficient recognition to warrant an invitation to establish a weekly lecture series organized by a group of men from multiple denominations. Starting in 1729, Gill dedicated himself to these Wednesday evenings for over twenty-six years. During this time, Gill adapted many of his lectures into print, including his *The Doctrine of The Trinity*, *The Cause of God and Truth*, and his *Exposition of the Old*

8   Rippon, *Memoir*, 37.
9   Rippon, *Memoir*, 65.

and New Testament. He finally resigned the lecture in 1756 in order to preserve his energy for the completion of his *Exposition of the Old Testament.*

Throughout the seventeenth century, the doctrine of the Trinity became a controversial doctrine and its denial led many away from the orthodox Christian faith. Gill, sensitive to the influence of these errors early in his ministry, used his Wednesday evening lectures to write *The Doctrine of the Trinity*, published in 1731. In this book, Gill sought to biblically prove the doctrine of the Trinity, setting down God's unity of essence and plurality of persons—Father, Son, and Spirit. The importance of defending this doctrine continued during Gill's ministry, evidenced by the book's republication in 1752. The issue of Trinitarian doctrine arose as an issue within Gill's church as they were required to disfellowship members who denied Christ's eternal Sonship. As a response, Gill proposed, and the church agreed, to add language to their statement of faith in order to more clearly define their Trinitarian convictions. And in the composition of his massive *Body of Doctrinal and Practical Divinity*, written in the very late stages of his life, Gill added substantial chapters to describe how each of the persons of the Trinity is distinguished from each other in the divine nature. Gill considered the Trinity a central doctrine that affects both one's belief and Christian experience.

Another of Gill's writings that emerged from the Great Eastcheap lectures and that defined his thinking was *The Cause of God and Truth*. Written and released in four parts between 1735–1738, Gill sought to respond to Daniel Whitby's *Discourse on the Five Points*. For Gill's part, he wrote to establish the theological and rational basis of Calvinism, as well as prove that church history did not favor the Arminian position. Even those who know little about Gill know something of his Calvinism. As Nettles has aptly written, "Seeking to convince people familiar with Baptist history that Gill fits within the frame of Calvinistic theology would be like trying to convince a veterinarian that cows give milk. 'Gill is a Calvinist' is a virtual redundancy.'"[10] Gill's belief in God's sovereign choice in election and salvation as a free gift of grace formed definitive features of his theological outlook.

---

10   Thomas J. Nettles, By His Grace and For His Glory: A Historical, *Theological and Practical Study of the Doctrines of Grace in Baptist Life* (Cape Coral, FL: Founders Press, 2006), 23.

As a pastor, Gill considered it his duty to feed his flock with God's word. Week in and week out for fifty-one years Gill went before his congregation and exposited God's word. The fruit of Gill's intense study, diligent preparation, and constant preaching of God's word became a massive and priceless gift to the church—a commentary on the entire Bible.

Each year, from 1746–1748, Gill published a successive volume of his *Exposition of the New Testament*. In recognition of Gill's accomplishment, Marischal College at Aberdeen University awarded Gill with a Doctorate of Divinity. Nearly a decade later in 1757 and 1758, Gill published an *Exposition of the Prophets* in two volumes, works which "gave him unfading honours, and induced such who have made those parts of the divine writings their study, to say, that if the words of Dr. Gill pre-eminently embrace almost every branch of sacred theology, *prophecy is his forte*."[11]

To complete his herculean *Exposition* of the whole Bible, Gill published the remainder of his Old Testament commentary in four volumes, each volume appearing in

11   Rippon, *Memoir*, 74.

successive years from 1763–1766. In total, his *Exposition* of both the Old and New Testament numbered nine volumes.

With a firm grasp of ancient history and the original languages, Gill's exposition is marked by historical and linguistic sensitivity. His expertise in rabbinical literature conspicuously appears throughout, but his exegetical writings are defined chiefly by his theological exegesis guided by the analogy of faith.

Near the end of his life, Gill spent more than five years preaching the substance of what would become his *Body of Doctrinal Divinity*. He published this two-volume work of systematic theology in 1769 and followed the next year with his *Body of Practical Divinity*, which he also composed of Sunday sermons. The creation of this *Body of Doctrinal and Practical Divinity* serves as the definitive statement of Gill's doctrine, and can be considered the fruit of his decades of exegesis and a symbol of his continuity with the Protestant scholastic tradition.

As Gill's physical abilities waned in his old age, his church suggested they hire a co-pastor. Gill replied with a letter of resignation, questioning the biblical warrant for co-pastors. Distressed by Gill's response, the church pleaded with him to remain as pastor, expressing that it was their "fixed desire, and Continual Prayer, that you may live and die in that endear'd Relation."[12] Gill remained their pastor until his death on October 14, 1771, having held that office more than fifty-one years.

Gill's significance today

From an historical perspective, Gill's legacy has received mixed reviews. While there are some who have cast him as the principal reason for Particular Baptist decline, others have lauded him as a defender of the faith who helped preserve the gospel amidst a decaying spiritual culture. Regardless of any negative effects related to his alleged hyper-Calvinism, Gill stood firmly against the winds of culture that so fiercely ravaged other denominations. In the face of Enlightenment rationalism, deism, and Unitarianism, Gill held firm to the inerrancy and authority of the Scriptures and defended the biblical doctrine of the Trinity. Gill's insistent confessionalism served as a stabilizing example during a time that Gill himself called "a day of darkness

---

12   George M. Ella, *John Gill and the Cause of God and Truth* (Durham: Go Publications, 1995), 240–242.

and gloominess." Regardless of where his culture stood, Gill stood on the unshakable foundation of Scripture.

In these and other respects, Gill stands as a spiritual example to follow. Whether one considers his life as a husband, father, or pastor, Gill exemplified a life of faithfulness and unshakable trust in Christ. Suffering the loss of numerous children in infancy, his daughter Elizabeth as a child, or his wife in old age, Gill fixed his heart firmly on the hope he held in Christ.

When Gill died he left behind the fruit of his faithful ministry in writing. In an estimated total of 10,000 pages, Christians today may still be taught by this Baptist luminary on a wide variety of topics ranging from linguistics to historical theology.

Gill's indefatigable study serves as an example to all Christians, but especially ministers. Gill so prized theological education he went to incredible lengths to teach himself Hebrew as well as other subjects. Gill never regretted these efforts that enriched his ministry and writings. So, too, will all Christians benefit from diligent study of God's word.

Jonathan E. Swan

What is theology?

In an era of the church marked by consumerism and pragmatism, the study of theology has fallen out of popularity among wide swaths of English-speaking Christians. The growing influence of a post-Christian culture and the prevalence of therapeutic, self-help versions of Christianity in the West have left little room for the study of theology. Seeming academic and impractical, it is no surprise that many Christians find little appreciation for theology.

This neglect of theology is not unique today, as this book will reveal. When John Gill wrote this introduction to theology, the entire enterprise had fallen on hard times. Gill, therefore, found it necessary to defend why he wrote, not just one book of theology, but three.

The excerpt-turned-book you now hold originally found its place in a large, three-volume work of theology. In its entirety titled *A Body of Doctrinal and Practical Divinity*, these three volumes attempted to scan the breadth of the Scripture's teaching on its main points. George Keith, John Gill's son-in-law, published the first two volumes in 1769 with the title *A Body of Doctrinal Divinity*. Gill published the third volume, *A Body of Practical Divinity*, in 1770.

Gill began this *Body of Divinity* with an Introduction, which has been excerpted into this book and given the title *What is Theology?* Academic works of theology that Gill's *Body of Divinity* resemble often begin with a "prolegomena," which serve as an extensive introduction that provides a rationale for the work's methodology and basis. Gill's Introduction functioned similarly to these theological prolegomena, but, like the rest of his writings, he directed it first and foremost to the church.

Gill viewed the *Body of Divinity* as a central part of his work as pastor when he followed up the publication of his *Exposition* of both the Old and New Testaments by preaching and then publishing his *Body of Divinity*.

For Gill, theology did not merely concern the halls of

academe. Theology, he believed, influenced the whole life of the individual Christian as well as the church. As his Introduction reveals, Gill considered theology to be essential for faithful Christianity. Right doctrine, Gill was convinced, leads to righteous living. This conviction shaped the very structure of his *Body of Doctrinal and Practical Divinity*. Following the pattern of the Apostle Paul, Gill began with doctrinal instruction in the *Body of Doctrinal Divinity*, which lead in turn to practical instruction in the *Body of Practical Divinity*. At the heart of Gill's thinking about theology was the belief that faithful theology in the heart of one who loves God guides the Christian towards God-glorifying godliness.

The reader of this book does not need to agree with all of Gill's methods or conclusions to appreciate his depth of insight, submission to Scripture, concern for holiness, and unflinching focus on Christ and his Gospel.

Published now more than three-hundred and fifty years ago, the fact that today you are reading this book attests to the continued importance of Gill's thought. Whether you are a Baptist like Gill or not, his writings offer you a scripturally-driven theology. In *What is theology?*, Gill continues to instruct his willing readers to carefully consider the task of studying God's word.

Jonathan E. Swan

WHAT

is

THEOLOGY?

JOHN GILL

INTRODUCTION

Having completed an exposition of the whole Bible, both the books of the Old and New Testaments, I considered with myself what would be best next to engage in for the further instruction of the people under my care. My thoughts led me to enter upon a scheme of doctrinal and practical divinity—first, the former, then the latter—the former being the foundation of the latter, and both having a close connection with each other.

Doctrine has influence upon practice; especially evangelical doctrine, spiritually understood, affectionately embraced, and powerfully and feelingly experienced. So true is what the apostle asserts: the grace of God has appeared to all men, Gentiles as well as Jews, in the external ministry of the word. This word is none other than the doctrine of the grace of God that brings salvation, the good news, the glad tidings of salvation by Christ, which is peculiar to gospel doctrine. We, to whom this word comes, are taught with power and efficacy in the demonstration of the Spirit, that "denying ungodliness and worldly lusts, we should live soberly, righteously, and godly in this present world."[1]

The purpose of theology

Where there is not the doctrine of faith, the obedience of faith cannot be expected. Where there is not the doctrine of the gospel, and men have not learned Christ, they live as if there was no God in the world and give themselves up to work all sin with greediness. And on the other hand, doctrine without practice, or a mere theory and speculative knowledge of things, unless reduced to practice, is of no avail. Such are only puffed up without reason in their sensuous minds; they profess to know God in word, but deny him by their works. These men have the appearance of godliness but denying its power, a name to live by but are dead.[2]

---

1   Titus 2:11–12.
2   Colossians 2:18; 2 Timothy 3:5; Titus 1:16; Revelation 3:1.

Doctrine and practice should go together. In order to know and do the will of God, instruction in doctrine and practice is necessary; the one being first taught will lead on to the other. The apostle Paul has pointed out this method of instruction to us in some of his epistles, especially in the epistle to the Ephesians. Here he first treats of election, predestination, adoption, acceptance in Christ, redemption and pardon of sin, regeneration, other doctrines of grace, and of the privileges of the saints under the gospel dispensation. He then enforces the several duties incumbent on them as men and Christians, respecting them in their several stations, in the church, in their families, and in the world.

So, the apostle instructed Timothy, first to "teach" the wholesome words of our Lord Jesus, the doctrine that is according to godliness and productive of it, and then to "exhort" and press men to the duties of religion from evangelical motives and principles. He also enjoined Titus to affirm the doctrines of the Gospel with constancy and certainty, to this end: "that those who have believed in God might be careful to maintain good works."[3]

---

3   See 1 Timothy 5:2–3; Titus 3:8.

And now having finished my scheme of doctrinal divinity, at the importunity of my friends I have been prevailed upon to publish it.

ONE

Theology is systematic

Systematical divinity, I am sensible, has become very unpopular. Formulas, articles of faith, creeds, confessions, catechisms, and summaries of divine truths are greatly decried in our age. Yet, what art or science has ever not been reduced to a system?

Systematics in other fields

Physics, metaphysics, logic, rhetoric, and even philosophy in general has had its several systems. Take notice of the various sects and systems of philosophy in ancient times. In the last age, the Cartesian system of philosophy was as greatly regarded as the Newtonian system is now. Astronomy, in particular, has been considered as a system, sometimes called the System of the Universe, and sometimes the Solar or Planetary System. The first system that is known is what was brought by Pythagoras (*c.*570–*c.*495 BC) into Greece and Italy, and from him called the Pythagorean System. This system was followed by many of the first and ancient philosophers. Though for many years it lay neglected, it has been lately revived, and is now much in vogue. The next is the Ptolemaic System, advanced by Ptolemy (*c.*100–*c.*170), which places the earth in the centre of the universe, and makes the heavens, with the sun, moon, and stars, to revolve about it. This was universally embraced for hundreds of years, until the Pythagorean System was revived by Nicolaus Copernicus (1473–1543), two or three hundred years ago, called henceforth the Copernican System.

In short, medicine, jurisprudence or law, and every art and science are reduced to a system or body, which is none other than an assemblage or composition of the several doctrines or parts of a science. Therefore, why should divinity, the most noble science, be without a system?

The purpose of systematizing

Evangelical truths are spread and scattered about in the

sacred Scriptures; to gather them together, and dispose of them in a regular orderly method, surely cannot be disagreeable. Such systemization of these truths is useful for the clarity and perspicuity of understanding them, for better retaining them in memory, and to show their connection, harmony, and agreement.

Accordingly, we find that Christian writers, in ancient times, attempted something of this nature. We see this in the several formulas of faith, symbols, or creeds made in the first three or four centuries of Christianity. Examples of systematizing include *The Stromata* by Clement of Alexandria (*c.*150–*c.*215), the four books of *On the First Principles* by Origen (*c.*184–*c.*253), *The Divine Institutes* by Lactantius (*c.*250–*c.*325), *The Great Catechism* by Gregory of Nyssa (*c.*335–*c.*395), the *Theological Orations* by Gregory of Nazianzus (329–390), *Commentary on the Apostles' Creed* by Tyrannius Rufinus (*c.*344–411), and the *Enchiridion* by Augustine of Hippo (354–430), with many others that followed.

Since the Reformation, we have had bodies or systems of divinity, and confessions of faith—the better digested versions of such systems—drawn up with greater accuracy and consistency. These have been very serviceable to lead men into the knowledge of evangelical doctrine, and confirm them in it, as well as to show the agreement and harmony of sound divines and churches, in the more principal parts of it. Even for those who now cry out against systems, confessions, and creeds, their own predecessors had systems of their own. Arius (*c.*256–336) had his creed, the Socinians have their *Racovian Catechism*, and the Remonstrants have published their confession of faith. Take notice of the several bodies of divinity published by Simon Episcopius (1583–1643), Philipp van Limborch (1633–1712), Etienne de Courcelles (1586–1659), and others. The Jews, in imitation of the Christians, have reduced their theology to certain heads or articles of faith. The chief Jewish systematician, if not the first that took this method, was the famous Moses Maimonides (1138–1204), who comprised their religious tenets in thirteen articles. After him Rabbi Joseph Albo (*c.*1380–1444), in his *Book of Principles*, reduced the articles of faith into three classes: the existence of God, the Law of Moses, and the doctrine of rewards and punishments.

Development of systematics

But what makes most for our purpose, and is worthy of our example, are the Scripture compendiums or systems of doctrine and duty. What better compendium or body of laws is the Decalogue or Ten Commandments, drawn up and calculated more especially for the use of the Jews, and suited to their circumstances! Such a body of laws cannot be equaled by the wisest legislators of Greece and Rome, Minos, Lycurgus, Zaleucus, and Numa. It cannot be equaled by the laws of The Twelve Tables[1] for order and regularity, for clearness and perspicuity, or for comprehensiveness and brevity. This body is divided into two tables in the most perfect order; the first respecting the worship of God and the duties owing to him, and the other respecting men and the mutual duties they owe to each other.

Prayer is a very principal and incumbent duty on men with respect to God. Yet, our Lord has given a very compendious directory, as to the matter of it, in what is commonly called the Lord's Prayer. This consists of petitions the most full, proper, and pertinent, and in the most regular order.

1   The foundation, or systematic formulation of Roman Law; this consolidation of law into twelve tables came about around 449 BC.

As to articles of faith or things to be believed, we have a creed. Hebrews 6:1–2 makes mention of this systematization according to six articles: repentance from dead works, faith towards God, the doctrine of baptism, the laying on of hands, the resurrection of the dead, and eternal judgment.

Doctrine always points to Christ

These are commonly thought to be so many articles of the Christian faith, but I rather think they are so many articles of the Jewish creed, embraced and professed by believers under the Jewish dispensation. The Christian Hebrews are directed to consider these articles as the principles of the doctrine of Christ, as an introduction, and as leading on to it, and which were in some sense to be left and not laid again.[2] They were not to stick and stop here, but to go on to perfection by searching into and embracing doctrines more sublime and perfect, as revealed in the gospel. They were not to be any longer instructed in the above articles in the manner they had been, but in a clearer manner—unattended with legal ceremonies—to view them and make

2   Hebrews 6:1.

48

use of them. Thus, for instance, the Christian Hebrews were not to learn the doctrine of repentance from slain beasts or to signify it by them, as they had been used to do. Every sacrifice brought for sin—which believers were no longer obliged to perform—was a tacit confession and an acknowledgment of sin. Their sacrifice of the creature evidenced that they repented of sin, acknowledging through the act that they deserved to die as the creature did. But now they were to exercise evangelical repentance in the view of a crucified Christ, and remission of sin by his blood. Whereas they had been taught to have faith towards God,[3] as the God of Israel, they were now moreover to believe in Christ as the Son of God, the true Messiah, the Savior of lost sinners, without the intervention of sacrifices. See John 14:1, "Let not your hearts be troubled. Believe in God; believe also in me."

The doctrine of baptism is to be understood of the diverse baptisms, or bathings among the Jews, spoken of in Hebrews 9:10 as "various washings and regulations for the body imposed until the time of reformation." These ordinances had a doctrine in them teaching the cleansing virtue

3   Hebrews 6:1.

of the blood of Christ, to be washed in his blood for sin and for uncleanness. At the coming of Christ, they were no longer to learn in this previous way, but to apply these ordinances immediately to the blood of Christ.

The doctrine of laying on of hands respects the laying on of the hands of the priests and people on the head of the sacrifices, which instructed in that great and evangelical truth, the transfer and imputation of sin to Christ, offered up in the room and stead of his people. This was to be taught and learnt no longer in that previous manner; Christ was made sin for his people, and had their sins imputed to him, which he bore in his own body on the tree.

As for the doctrines of the resurrection of the dead and eternal judgment, they were such as distinguished Jews and Gentiles, which the latter were greatly strangers to a future state. Though they were common to Jews and Christians, yet the believing Hebrews were not to rest in the knowledge they had of these, as enjoyed under the former dispensation, but to go on to a perfected doctrine. They were to press forward towards a greater share of knowledge of these doctrines and of other more sublime doctrines. Life and immortality were brought to light by Christ in a clearer and brighter manner through the gospel.

All systematics lead to the gospel

But all that I mean by this is that the principal doctrines of faith under the Jewish dispensation are reduced to a system, though this system was meant to be improved and perfected under the gospel dispensation. Those previous articles were but few; though Gregory the Great observes, that according to the increase of times, the knowledge of saints increased. The nearer they were to the coming of the Savior, the more fully they perceived the mysteries of salvation.[4] The articles in the formulas and symbols of the first Christians were but few, suitable to the times in which they lived, and as opposite to the errors then broached. They were increased by new errors that sprung up, which made an increase of articles necessary, otherwise the same articles of faith were believed by the ancients as by later posterity. Thomas Aquinas (1225–1274) concludes this subject by saying:

4   Gregory the Great, Homily 16 on Ezekiel: "The knowledge of the holy fathers increased as time went on ... and the nearer they were to our Savior's coming, the more fully did they receive the mysteries of salvation."

Articles of faith have increased by succession of times, not indeed as to the substance, but as to the explanation and express profession of them. What are explicitly, and under a greater number, believed by posterity, all the same were believed by the fathers before them, implicitly and under a lesser number.

It is easy to observe that the first summaries of faith, recorded by the most ancient writers, went no further than the doctrine of the trinity, or what concerns the three divine persons; the doctrines of the heretics of the first ages being opposed to one or other of these articles. Yet, when other heresies sprung up and other false doctrines were taught, it became necessary to add new articles, to explain, defend, and secure truth, as well as to distinguish those who were found in the faith of the gospel from those that were not.

TWO

Interpreting doctrine

Mention is made in the New Testament of a "form of doctrine delivered"[1] and a "form of sound words" that had been heard and was to be held fast,[2] and of a proportion or analogy of faith, according to which ministers were to prophesy or preach. The first of these mentions is spoken of in Romans 6:17: "Yet you obeyed from the heart that form of doctrine which was delivered to you." This "form of sound words" is not to be understood as the specific Scriptures or written word delivered to them, but of the gospel and the doctrines of it preached by the apostle in the ministry of the word to the Romans. Through this form of preaching,

1   Romans 6:17.
2   2 Timothy 1:13.

those first hearers had yielded to the obedience of faith. The "form of doctrine delivered" is understood as a type, or pattern, and so the word is rendered as a pattern to which the hearers are to conform their faith and practice.[3] Likewise, 2 Timothy 1:13 refers to a pattern of sound teaching which was heard by preaching. The use of *word* in Ephesians 1:13 is of a form exactly expressed, always to be had in view, to be attended to, and followed. Through delineation of the term here translated, we understand it as a picture, or the outline of a portrait given by painters to their learners, always to be looked to and imitated. The apostle Paul proposed a form either in private conversation or through public ministry, carefully respecting such information as a rule to faith and practice. Though the apostle reduced the gospel doctrines to a system, even this form was collected out of the Scriptures, confirmed by them, and agreeable to them.

The apostle Paul reduces his ministry to these two heads, "repentance towards God," and "faith towards the Lord" Jesus Christ.[4] According to these two heads, he delivers a rich summary, a glorious compendium, and a chain of

---

3   See Hebrews 8:5; 1 Timothy 4:12.
4   Acts 20:21.

gospel truths through Romans 8:30. This passage is worthy, as a form and pattern, to gospel ministers to attend to, and according to it to regulate their ministrations.

The analogy of faith

Once more, the apostle speaks of a proportion or an analogy of faith, "if prophesy, let us prophesy according to the proportion of faith."[5] John Calvin (1509–1564), on the text observes, by such faith is meant the first axioms of religion, to which whatsoever doctrine is not found to answer is convicted of falsehood. And so Johannes Piscator (1546–1625) writes concerning the terminology of the analogy of faith. He explains that the interpretation of Scripture we bring is analogous to the articles of faith, that is, agreeing with them and consenting to them, and not repugnant to their true meaning. Similarly, David Parseus (1548–1622), on the text, is more express saying:

> Analogy, is not the same as "measure" (Romans 12:3) for measure is of one thing measured, but analogy

5   Romans 12:6.

is between two things that are analogous. Here, the apostle seems to describe something more, namely, to prescribe a rule by which all prophesying is to be directed; therefore by faith others understand the rule of Scripture and the axioms of faith, such as are comprehended in the Symbol of the Apostolic faith (or the Apostles' Creed) which have in them a manifest truth from the Scriptures. "Analogy" is the evident harmony of faith and consent of the heads (or articles) of faith, to which whatever agrees is true, and whatever disagrees is false and adulterate. This is the rule of all prophesying (or preaching); therefore, according to the rule of the sacred Scripture and the Apostles' Creed, all interpretations, disputations, questions, and opinions in the church, are to be examined, that they may be conformable thereunto.

And though what is now called the Apostles' Creed might not be composed by them, nor so early as their time; yet the substance of it was agreeable to their doctrine, and therefore called theirs. This Creed was a rule of faith, very near the apostle's teaching in words, received, embraced, and professed very early in the Christian church. Tertullian (*c.*155–*c.*220) gives further elaboration through the following words:

> The rule of faith is truly one, solely immoveable and irreformable (not to be corrected and mended); namely, of believing in the only God Almighty, the maker of the world, and in his Son Jesus Christ, born of the virgin Mary, crucified under Pontius Pilate, raised from the dead on the third day, received into heaven, sitting now at the right hand of the Father, who will come to judge the quick and dead by or at the resurrection of the dead.

And such a set of principles, as or what are similar to them and accord with the word of God, may be called the analogy of faith. And a late writer observes on the word analogy,

> The analogy of faith, our divines call the sum of heavenly doctrine concerning articles of faith, taken out of such passages of Scripture, where, as in their proper

place, they are treated of in clear and plain words.[6]

Upon the whole, it seems no ways incongruous with the sacred writings, but perfectly agreeable to them, that articles and heads of faith, or a summary of gospel truths, may be collected from them. Such a collection of doctrines is useful to declare explicitly our belief of them, to strengthen the faith of others in them, to show our agreement in them with other Christians in the principal parts, and to distinguish ourselves from those who oppose the faith once delivered to the saints.

Confessions and the bare words of Scripture

It is strongly pleaded, that articles and confessions of faith, in which men are to agree, should be expressed in the bare words of the sacred Scriptures, and that nothing should be considered as a fundamental article that is a matter of controversy. As to the latter, if that was admitted, there would be scarce any article at all left us to believe. What is there out of almost all that is believed, which is not controverted

6   Noted from Christiani Stockii (anonymous) in *Clavis Linguae Sanctae* (Jena, Germany: Felicem Bielckium, 1730).

by some? Or is there any passage of Scripture brought in support of a particular doctrine, for which the sense of it is not called in question, or perverted? Just as Clement of Alexandria says, "I do not think there is any Scripture so happy as to be contradicted by none."

As to the former, let us consider our being tied up to the bare words of Scripture concerning any doctrine of faith delivered in them. We ought to entertain the highest esteem of the words of Scripture and have the greatest value for them; they are clothed with such majesty, and having such an energy in them, which the words of man's wisdom and teaching do not have. However, our sense of these bare Scripture words cannot be expressed but in words literally varying from them. Also, it should be settled what is meant by bare words of Scripture, whether of the original text, Hebrew and Greek, or of any translation in our modern tongues. If the words of a translation, a man cannot be sure that this always does express the sense of Scripture, especially in difficult and hotly debated passages. If of the original, then both he that makes the confession, and they to whom it is made, ought to understand Hebrew and Greek; and even every member of a church where a confession of faith is required in order to join in communion. If a rule of faith and practice is to be made in the bare words of Scripture, even if it is in the words of a translation—without an explanation of the sense of these words in our modern understanding of the words, it might introduce into a Christian community all sorts of errors that can be named, which would be utterly inconsistent with its peace, concord, harmony, and union.

Scripture's interpretation requires words

Moreover, to be obliged to express ourselves only in the words of Scripture would be to destroy all exposition and interpretation of Scripture. Without words different from, though agreeable to, the sacred Scriptures, we can never express our sense of them, nor explain them to others according to the sense we have entertained of them. Though no Scripture is of private interpretation, or a man's own interpretation—as if to obligate others to believe another man's faith—yet by utilizing bare words will become of no interpretation at all, private or public, of a man's own or of others. Indeed, it is sometimes said that "Scripture is the best interpreter of Scripture," and which in some respects is true; as when, for the better understanding of a passage of

Scripture, another more clear and explicit truth is set to it and compared with it, and which serves to throw light on it and give a clearer discernment of it, and of its true sense. However, that light, discernment, and sense which comes through Scripture cannot be expressed but in words literally different from them both.

Scripture's interpretation requires reason

To be obliged to express ourselves about divine things in the bare words of Scripture tends to make the ministry and preaching of the word useless in great measure. By such exercise, a minister of the word would have nothing else to do but to read a string of select passages of Scripture relating to any particular subject. He would then deliver this reading without attempting any illustration, or making use of any reasonings to explain or strengthen the points of doctrine contained in them. Even so in common, the hearers of that minister may as well stay at home and read the Scriptures in their private houses, rather than to attend on public ministrations.

Surely the apostle Paul, in his reasonings, explanations, and allegations, must have used his own words when he opened the Scriptures, "explaining and proving that it was necessary for the Christ to suffer and to rise from the dead," and that this Jesus whom he preached was Christ.[7] Though his words accorded with the Scriptures, those words must literally vary from them when he reasoned, elucidated, and confirmed his arguments concerning the messiahship of Jesus, his suffering of death, and resurrection from the dead. Yet he said nothing else as to the substance than what Moses and the prophets said concerning Christ, yet in words different from theirs. According to this opposing scheme, all public ministrations must be at an end, as well as all writing in defense of truth and for the confutation of errors.

Yes, this must in a great measure cramp all religious conversation about divine things, if not destroy it. What purpose is there for those who fear God to meet frequently and speak to one another about the things of God and truths of the gospel, if they are not to make use of their own words to express their sense of these things by them? How, in this way, can Christian meetings be to mutual edification? How can Christians build up one another in their most holy

7   Acts 17:3.

faith? How can weaker and less experienced Christians receive any advantage from more knowing and stronger ones, if only they are to declare their sense of things in the bare words of Scripture?

Indeed, John Owen (1616–1683) presents an argument against this case of solely using bare words. As it would be unlawful to speak or write otherwise than in the words of Scripture, so it would be unlawful to think or conceive in the mind anything other than what the Scripture expresses. The whole of what Owen says on this subject is worth repeating:

> To deny the liberty, yes, the necessity hereof, (that is, of making use of such words and expressions, as it may be, are not literally and formally contained in Scripture, but only are to our conceptions and apprehensions expository of what is so contained) is to deny all interpretation of the Scripture, all endeavors to express the sense of the words of Scripture to the understanding of another, which is, in a word, to render the Scripture itself altogether useless. If it is unlawful for me to speak or write what I conceive to

be the sense of the words of Scripture and the nature of the thing signified and expressed by them, it is unlawful for me also to think or conceive in my mind what is the sense of the words or nature of the things. This is to make brutes of ourselves, and to frustrate the whole design of God in giving to us the great privilege of his word.[8]

Scripture's interpretation through expression

The sentiments of one man in any point of religion cannot be distinguished from those of another, though diametrically opposite were only the words of Scripture to be the determining factor. In this way, the words of an Arian cannot be known from an Athanasian. Both the Arian and Athanasian will say, in the words of Scripture, that Christ is the "great God," the "true God," and "over all God blessed forever," but without expressing themselves in their own words, their different sentiments will not be discerned. Truly, the Arian holds that Christ is a created God, of a like but not of the same substance with his Father. Using the same

8   John Owen, *A Brief Declaration and Vindication of the Doctrine of the Trinity*, (London: R.W. for Nath. Ponder, 1669), 30–31.

Scripture phrasing, the Athanasian expresses that Christ is equal with the Father, of the same nature, substance, and glory. The person who believes the latter, surely it cannot be unlawful to express his belief of it in such words which declare the true sense of his mind.

To further this example, a Sabellian (who is also called a Unitarian) and a Trinitarian will not scruple to say in Scripture terms what Christ says of himself and his Father, "I and my Father are one." However, the Sabellian holds Christ and the Father are one in person or but one person; whereas the Trinitarian affirms Christ and the Father are one in nature and essence, but two distinct persons. Surely, it must be lawful for the Trinitarian to express himself, if this is the real sentiment of his mind. Much in this same way, a Socinian and an anti-Socinian will join in saying that Christ is the "Word who is God," that he is the "only begotten of the Father," and the "only begotten Son of God." The Socinian maintains, by these Scripture phrases, that Christ is only God by office, not by nature, and that he is the only begotten Son of God by office or by adoption. The anti-Socinian professes the same verses to prove that Christ is God by nature, and that he is the Son of the Father by natural and eternal generation, being begotten by him.

It is necessary, therefore, that these teachers of the Bible should make use of their own words to express their sentiments, otherwise, how should it be known that they differ from one another? Indeed, this seems to be the grand reason why it is urged by some with so much vehemence that only Scripture words and phrases should be made use of. These crafty teachers assert this sentiment so that their erroneous tenets may not be detected and exposed. As a learned man has observed, those who would nourish and cherish their monstrous and heretical notions are the very same who cavil at any expression of formulas (of sound doctrine used by the orthodox). These men would plead concerning any pattern or system that they should be very short, and composed in the bare words of Scripture. Let the reader note, is this not the experience of which all ages testify? Sometimes such persons take detached passages of Scripture from different places and join them together, though they have no connection and agreement with each other. This is the same method Irenaeus (*c*.130–*c*.202) observes the ancient heretics took, who made use of passages of Scripture, that their figments might not seem to be without a testimony, but passed over the order and connection of the Scriptures, and loosened the parts of truth as much as in them lay. These are they who fitly compare such to one who should take the effigy of a king made of jewels and precious stones by a skillful artificer, and loosen and separate them, and of them make the form of a dog or a fox.

Examining words of Scripture

It does not appear that those men, who are so strenuous for the use of Scripture phrases only in articles of religion, have a greater value for the Scriptures than others—nay, not so much. If we are to form a judgment of them by their sermons and writings, one would think they never read the Scriptures at all, or very little, since they make such an infrequent use of them. You will scarcely hear a passage of Scripture quoted by them in a sermon, or produced by them in their writings; more frequently Lucius Annaeus Seneca (*c*.4 BC–AD 65), Marcus Tullius Cicero (106–43 BC), and others. It looks as if they thought it very impolite, and that it might only disgrace their more refined writings were they to fill their performances with Scripture. After all, it is easy to observe that these men—the Arians formerly, and the Socinians more lately—carry on their cause, and endeavor to support it by making use of unscriptural words and phrases. Therefore, it is not with a very good grace that such men, or those of the same cast with them, object to the use of words and phrases not syllabically expressed in Scripture. Aside from all these arguments, we can easily note that it was the Arians who first began to make use of unscriptural phrases, as Athanasius I of Alexandria (*c.*298–373) affirms! The Athanasians had as much a right to use the word *homoousios* as the Arians had to use *homoioousios*. The Athanasians could then explain their sense of the word and defend their doctrine concerning the person of Christ and his equality with God, and did so against the Arians who introduced a phrase subversive of it. The Calvinists have as good authority to make use of the word "satisfaction" in the doctrine of expiation of sin and atonement for it, as the Socinians and Remonstrants have for the use of the word "acceptilation," whereby they seek to obscure and weaken it.

Words and phrases, though not literally expressed in Scripture, yet if what is meant by them is to be found there, they may be lawfully made use of. Some examples of these are plainly expressed respecting the doctrine of the trinity. See the examples used in treating of that doctrine, as "nature,"[9] "Godhead,"[10] and "Person"—that is, the person of the Father, and the person of Christ.[11] Other examples are clearly signified by "essence,"[12] by the name of God, "I am what I am,"[13] the "unity" of divine persons,[14] a "Trinity" of Persons in the unity of essence,[15] and the "generation" of the Son by and of the Father.[16] Other peculiar doctrines respecting revelation, the state of men, and the grace of Christ may as well be deduced from Scripture.[17] Clarity is also given to the form of doctrine in "imputation of Adam's sin" to his posterity,[18] as well as the "imputation of Christ's righteousness" to them that believe, which is nearly syllabically

---

9   Galatians 4:8.

10   Colossians 2:9.

11   2 Corinthians 2:10; Hebrews 1:3.

12   2 Corinthians 4:6.

13   Exodus 3:14.

14   John 10:30.

15   1 John 5:7.

16   Psalm 2:7.

17   John 1 :14, 18.

18   Romans 5:19.

expressed in the text.[19] What is more, the term "imputation" is explained according to that sin imputed to Christ, who "was made sin," by imputation.[20] And we read of the "satisfaction" of Christ for sin by all that is implied in those places where it is signified what Christ has done and suffered in the room and stead of his people, this according to the content of law and justice, and that God is well pleased with it.

The importance of definitions

These are the principal words and phrases objected to, and which we will not be prevailed upon to part with easily. And indeed, words and phrases, the use and sense of these words and phrases have long been acknowledged in the churches of Christ. Indeed, these words and phrases are well known, and they have served aptly to convey the sense to those that use them. It is unreasonable to require the Church to part with them, unless others, and those better words and phrases, are substituted in their room.

However, such words and phrases as are proposed should not be easily admitted without strict examination,

19   Romans 4:6.
20   2 Corinthians 5:21.

for there is oftentimes a good deal of truth in that saying, "he that coins new words, coins new doctrines;" so we see the need for strict examination in the notorious case of Arius. We read that Arius' own bishop, Alexander I of Alexandria (d.328), charged him with saying things without Scripture, and what was never said before. As an example, Arius claimed that God was not always a Father, but that there was a time when he was not a Father. He likewise claimed that the Word did not always exist, but was made out of things that were created, and so there was a time when Christ was not a Son. Eusebius (c.260–c.340), who favored Arius' views, also owns that the inspired writings never used such phrases, that Christ was "from non-entities," from things that are not (i.e. was made out of nothing). Eusebius notes that the phrase, "there was a time when he was not," was not something they had ever been used to.

THREE

Defining the word theology

The subject of the following work being theology, or what we call divinity, it is now proper to consider the signification and use of the word, and from where it has its rise. I say, *what we call divinity*, because it seems to be a word of which the use in such subject matter is peculiar to us. Foreign writers never entitle their works of this kind, as a body, system, or marrow of *divinity*, but they use the terms of a body, system, or marrow of *theology*. The word divinity comes from a word used only by Latin writers for deity or godhead; however, we need not scruple with the use of it. Custom and use among us have long fixed the sense of the word to signify, when used on this subject, a treatise on the science of divine things, sacred truths, and Christian doctrines, taken out of the Scriptures. The Jews seem to come nearest to us in the phrase which they use concerning it, calling it a science of divinity, or a divine science; that is, a science or doctrine concerning divine things, concerning God, concerning his divinity, and things belonging to him. So we see that mainly, this use is the same in sense with the word theology, as will be seen hereafter.

Jewish theology

Before we proceed any further, it may not be improper to observe the distinction of the Jewish theology, or the two parts into which they divide it. The first branch they call the work of *bereshith* or the creation, named so because *bereshith* is the first word in Genesis 1:1, "In the beginning God created." They frequently use this term to signify the whole work of the creation, so this part of their theology respects the creatures God has made, and the nature of them whereby the invisible things of God, as the apostle says, are discerned, even his eternal power and Godhead. This branch is their physics or natural theology. The other branch is called the work of the chariot; such an appellation is taken from the vision in Ezekiel 1:1–28 of the four living creatures in the form of a chariot. This is the more abstruse and mysterious part of their theology and may be called their metaphysics or supernatural theology. This branch treats of God, his divine attributes, of the Messiah, of angels, and the souls of men. Similar teaching as pertains to this branch may be found in the *Zohar*, and other cabalistic writings. But to go on.

The Greek development of terms

Theology is a Greek word, and signifies a discourse concerning God and things belonging to him. It was first in use among the heathen poets and philosophers, and from them came the word *theologue* as one who gives discourse on the things concerning God or the gods. Lactantius says, the most ancient writers of Greece were called *theologues*; these were their poets who wrote of their deities, and of the genealogies of them. Pherecydes of Syros (*c.*580 BC–*c.*560 BC) is said to be the first that wrote of divine things; so Thales says, in his letter to Pherecydes, hence he had the name of *theologue*. However, some make Musaeus of Athens,[1] the

---

1   Considered the founder of priestly poetry in Attica.

son of Eumolphus, the first of this sort, and others give the title to Orpheus. Pythagoras, the disciple of Pherecydes, has also this appellation; this comes from Porphyry of Tyre (*c*.234 BC–*c*.305 BC) who, by way of eminence, calls him the *theologue*. Even so, Porphyry, in his writings, speaks often of the *theologues*. Likewise, Plato was given this character while Aristotle makes mention of the *theologues*, as distinct from naturalists, or the natural philosophers, Cicero also speaks of them, and seems to design by them the poets, or the authors of mystic theology. The Egyptians had their theology, which they communicated to Darius, the father of Xerxes. From developments through such communications come the Magi and the Chaldeans, of whom Democritus (*c*.460 BC–*c*.370 BC) is said to learn theology and astrology. The priests of Delphos are called by Plutarch (46 BC–*c*.119 BC), the *theologues* of Delphos.

It is from here that these words theology and *theologues* have been borrowed, and made use of by Christian writers; and I see no impropriety in the use of them, nor should they be thought the worse of for their origination—at least no more than other words which come from the heathen sources. Though these words are used of false deities, and by persons that write or speak of them, it should not follow that they may not be used with great propriety, of discourses concerning the true God, things belonging to him, and of those that discourse on such things.

The first among Christians that has the title of *theologue*, or divine, is St. John, the writer of the book of the Revelation; for so the inscription of the book runs "the Revelation of St. John the Divine." In the Complutensian Polyglot edition, and so in the King of Spain's Bible, it is "the Revelation of the holy Apostle and Evangelist, John the Divine." Whether this word *theologue* or divine was originally in the inscription of this book I will not say, yet Origen, a very early Christian writer, gives to John the title of the divine, as it should seem from here. Athanasius, in his account of the sacred writings, calls the book of Revelation, "the Revelation of John the Divine," and also styles him, "John the Evangelist and Divine." These words *theologue* and theology are to be met with frequently in the ancient Fathers, in following ages, and in all Christian writers to the present times.

The science of God
Upon the whole, it appears that theology, or divinity, as

we call it, is no other than a science or doctrine concerning God, or a discoursing and treating of things relating to him. A *theologue*, or a divine, is one that understands, discourses, and treats of divine things. Perhaps the Evangelist John might have this title eminently given to him by the ancients because of his writing concerning, and the record he bore to Christ, the Logos, the essential Word of God, to his proper deity, divine sonship, and distinct personality. Suidas (tenth century) not only calls him the divine and the Evangelist, but says that he wrote theology, by which he seems to mean the book of the Revelation, which book some have observed contains a complete body of divinity. Here we are taught the divine authority and excellency of the sacred Scriptures, that there is but one God, and that he only is to be worshipped, and not angels. We are taught that God is the triune God; that there are three persons in the Godhead, Father, Son, and Holy Spirit; that God is eternal, the Creator, and Preserver of all things; that Christ is truly God and truly man; that he is Prophet, Priest, and King; that men are by nature wretched, blind, naked, poor, and miserable; that some of all nations are redeemed by the blood of the Lamb; and that they are justified and washed from their sins in his blood. Observed in this writing are the articles of the resurrection of the dead, the last judgment, the sad estate of the wicked, and the happiness of the saints.

As we are upon this subject, it may not be amiss if we take a brief compendious view of the state of theology; or, if you please, divinity, from the beginning of it to the present time. Theology may be considered either as natural or supernatural. By natural we mean that which is understood from the light of nature, and that which is attained through the use and exercise of it. By supernatural we mean that which is come at by divine revelation.

FOUR

Natural theology

Natural theology may be considered either as it was in Adam before the fall, or as in him and his posterity since the fall.

Natural theology before the Fall

Adam, before the fall, had great knowledge of things divine as well as natural, moral, and civil. He was created in the image of God, which image lay in knowledge, as well as in righteousness and holiness. Before he came short of this glory and lost this image, or at least was greatly impaired and obliterated in him by sin, he knew much of God, of his nature and attributes, of his mind and will, and the worship of him. Adam had knowledge of the persons in God, of a trinity of persons who were concerned in the creation of all things, and in his own; and without which he could have had no true knowledge of God, nor have yielded the worship due to each divine person. Adam was assisted in this knowledge of God, as it was not innate within himself or sprung from the light of nature within himself. This knowledge was capable of being increased by things outside of man, such as by symbols, the tree of life in the midst of the garden, and so on. Just as well, Adam increased in knowledge by the positive precepts relating to the worship of God, and obedience to his will, as the prohibition to eat of the tree of knowledge of good and evil, the institution of marriage, and through a constant and diligent contemplation of the works of creation.

We cannot suppose him to be altogether without the benefit and advantage of divine revelation since he had such a near and immediate intercourse and converse with God himself. There is much Adam could not have known without the intervention of God. Adam learned from God as to the creation of the world, the order and manner of it, of his own formation out of the dust of the earth and the formation of Eve from him, that Eve was flesh of his flesh and bone of his bone, and that she was designed of God to be his wife, and a helper to him, and that she was to be the mother of all living. Through God's personal revelation, Adam also grew in knowledge respecting the worship of God, the manner of it, and the covenant made with him as a federal head to all his posterity that should spring from him. These, with many other things, no doubt, Adam had immediate knowledge of from God himself.

But this kind of theology appeared with a different aspect in Adam after his fall, and in his posterity. By sin his mind was greatly clouded, and his understanding darkened. According to the curse of the fall, Adam lost much of his knowledge of God, and of his perfections. Were this sudden absence of knowledge not true, then he would never have imagined that going among the trees of the garden would hide him from the presence of God, and secure him from God's justice. What a notion must he have of the omnipresence of God? Consider also of his perspective of God's omniscience, when he attempted to palliate and cover his sin by the excuse he made. And he immediately lost his familiar intercourse with God, and communion with him, being drove out of the garden.

Theology apart from revelation

As for Adam's posterity, descending from him by ordinary generation, they appear to be in the same case and circumstances, without God in the world, without any true knowledge of him, or fellowship with him. These children appear to be in the image of the earthly and sinful Adam, and not to have the image of God upon them; they are alienated from the life of God, and their understandings darkened as to the knowledge of divine and spiritual things. Though there are some remains of the light of nature in them, by which something of God may be known by them, yet whatever they know of him in theory, which does not amount to a true knowledge of God, they are without a practical knowledge of him. Even by considering the works of creation, they could observe his eternal power and Godhead—to do otherwise is inexcusable—but they do not glorify him as God, and instead serve the creature more than the Creator. Yes, what knowledge they have of God is very dim and obscure. They are like persons in the dark, who grope about, if happily they may feel after him, and find him. And what ridiculous notions they entertained of deity. And what gods they manufactured to reign over themselves!

The children of Adam fell into impiety and idolatry, polytheism and atheism. They were left without divine revelation, without the true knowledge of the worship of God, and therefore they introduced strange and absurd modes of worship. They were at a loss as to what methods to take to reconcile with God, and yet continued to offend with their sins whenever it would have been sensible to repent. They were truly at a loss as to what means and ways they could make use of to recommend themselves to him, and therefore they went into practices most shocking and detestable to God. Being destitute of divine revelation, they had no assurance that God would pardon sin and sinners, nor had they any knowledge of his way of justifying sinners by the righteousness of his Son—such are doctrines of pure revelation. They had no knowledge of Christ as Mediator, the way of peace and reconciliation, of life and salvation by him, and so they had no true knowledge of God in Christ. As Scripture says, "this is eternal life, that they know you, the only true God, and Jesus Christ whom you have sent."[1] There is no saving knowledge of God without Christ, therefore the

---

1   John 17:3.

light of nature is insufficient to salvation. Though men may arrive at the knowledge of a God as the Creator of all things, yet they cannot come to the knowledge of Christ as the Savior of men without faith in him; without this revelation there can be no salvation.

Weakness of natural theology

Though by means of natural theology men may know in some instances what is displeasing to God, what is agreeable to him, what is to be avoided, and what is to be performed, yet even in the things they do know, they do not answer to their knowledge in their practice. In their natural knowledge they are yet deficient, reckoning such things to be no sins which are grievous ones, as fornication, polygamy, suicide, etc. Even if these men were to be diligent in keeping clear of such sins, they would not be saved merely by obedience. If by obedience to the law of Moses none are justified and saved, then certainly none will be saved by obedience to the law and light of nature. None can be saved without faith in Christ, and his righteousness. There is no pardon but by his blood and no acceptance with God but through him—such truths are those which the light of nature leaves keeps men strangers to. Perhaps more may be said of the weakness and insufficiency of natural theology to instruct men in the knowledge of divine things—as to those destitute of any divine revelation—when the theology of the pagans may be observed.

FIVE

Supernatural theology

Supernatural theology, or what is by pure revelation, may now be considered in its original rise and progress; and as it has been improved and increased, or has met with checks and obstructions.

Adam to Noah

The state of this theology may be considered as it was from the first appearance of it, after the fall of Adam, to the flood in the times of Noah, or throughout the old world. When God pronounced to the serpent, "It (the seed of the woman) shall bruise your head, and you shall bruise his heel,"[1]

---

1   Genesis 3:15.

this stirred humanity to study theology, and is the foundation of such study. God's pronouncement contains the principal articles of Christian theology; as the incarnation of the Messiah, the Savior of men, who should be "the seed of the woman," made of a woman, made flesh, and become a partaker of the flesh and blood of those he was to save. This seems to be understood by our first parents; it is thought that Eve imagined that this illustrious person was born of her when she brought forth her firstborn, saying, "I have gotten a man by the Lord,"[2] as some choose to render the word. In the same expectation, Enos, the son of Seth, was expected to be the Redeemer of the world, according to the Cabalists. Due to this anticipation of fulfillment, the next child was called Enos, "the man," the famous excellent man, as they say.

Likewise, this pronouncement shows forth the sufferings and death of Christ in the human nature, by means of the serpent Satan. This promised one will tread upon Satan, even while he, like a serpent, would turn himself and bite the promised seed's heel. This heel is understood to express

2   Genesis 4:1.

the human nature of the man who Satan is wrapped around. That the serpent would strike his heel, that is to strike the man in his inferior nature, and so bring him to the dust of death. However, the Messiah, by his sufferings and death, would bruise the serpent's head, confound his schemes, destroy his works, and yes, destroy him who is the devil, and who had the power of death. By the seed's treading the head of the serpent he abolishes that power over death; yes, he makes an end of sin which is the cause of death, by giving full satisfaction for it. Through this verse, the promised seed would so save and deliver his people from all the sad effects of sin, eternal wrath, ruin, and damnation.

This kind of theology received some further improvement from the coats of skin with which the Lord God made and clothed our first parents. Though mere animal skins, these coats are an emblem of the justifying righteousness of Christ, and of the garments of salvation wrought out by his obedience, sufferings, and death. Through this emblem signified by slain beasts, God puts upon his people this salvation, and clothes them with justifying righteousness through his gracious act of imputation—here they are said to be "justified by blood." Another theological picture may be added in the flow of revelation which is the hieroglyph of the cherubim and flaming sword, placed at the end of the garden to observe or point at the tree of life. This hieroglyph represents the prophets of the Old, and the apostles and ministers of the New Testament, placed and appointed to show to men the way of salvation by Christ the tree of life.

And what serves to throw more light on this evangelical theology, are the sacrifices ordered to be offered. These offerings are types of the sacrifice of Christ. The sacrifice which most particularly enlightens evangelical theology is what was offered up by Abel, who, "by faith" in the sacrifice of Christ, "offered up a more excellent sacrifice than Cain."[3] This sacrifice was also a lamb, the firstling of his flock, and pointed at the Lamb of God, who by his sacrifice takes away the sins of his people. During this period, men seem to have increased in light, as to the worship of God, especially public worship. In the times of Enos, the grandson of Adam, men "began to call upon the name of the Lord."[4] Prayer to God, and invocation of his name, were used before—no

3   Hebrews 11:4.
4   Genesis 4:26.

doubt—but as men increased, and families became more numerous, they now met and joined together in carrying on social and public worship. Though there were those who called on the name of the Lord, yet there grew more corruptions in practice, within this period of time. Wicked Cain, whose works were evil, set a bad example to his posterity, leading them to indulge themselves in the gratification of sinful pleasures. Cain's posterity, though separate from the posterity of Seth, yet lived together with them. It is said that, in the times of Jared, some descended from the holy mountain, as it is called, to the company of Cain, in the valley, and mixed themselves with them, and took of their daughters for wives. Through this sexual immorality sprung a race of giants and wicked men, who were the cause of the flood. Lamech gave into the practice of bigamy. Pseudo-Berossus (third century BC) says that Ham lived a very vicious and profligate life before the flood. Yet even with all of this sinful behavior, there does not appear to have been any corruption in doctrine and worship, or any idolatry exercised. Some indeed have pretended that in the days of Enos images were invented, to excite the minds of creatures to pray to God by them as mediators, but this is said without any foundation.

Noah to Moses

The next period of time in which supernatural theology may be traced, is from the flood in the times of Noah, to the giving of the law to Israel in the times of Moses. Noah was instructed in theology by his father Lamech, who expected great comfort from his son.[5] Some think Lamech instructed Noah in spiritual as well as in civil things, but whatever the case he was certainly instructed in the true religion, as it was received from the first man, Adam. This theology was taught to Noah, and the knowledge of it conveyed to his posterity, and even partly in the ministry of the word by him. Noah was a "preacher of righteousness," even of evangelical righteousness, "of the righteousness of faith," of which he was an heir, and therefore no doubt preached the same to others.[6] He taught, as well, partly by the sacrifices he offered, which were of clean creatures concerning which he had the knowledge of the distinctions revealed to him. These sacrifices were of a sweet savor to God, and were typical of the purity of Christ's sacrifice for sin, and of the acceptance of it to God, which is to him of a sweet smelling savor.

5   Genesis 5:29.
6   Hebrews 11:7.

Moreover, the waters of the flood, and the ark in which Noah and his family were preserved, were a type of an evangelical ordinance, the ordinance of baptism. This baptism is an emblem of the death, burial, and resurrection of Christ, by which men are saved.[7] When Noah and his family went into the ark, the fountains of the great deep were broken up below, and the windows of heaven opened above, thus they were like persons covered in water, immersed in it, and buried there. When they came out of it, the water being carried off, it was like a resurrection, and as life from the dead. This is indicated by "the like figure," or "antitype" as the apostle says, "which now saves us—baptism (not the removal of the flesh, but the answer of a good conscience toward God), through the resurrection of Jesus Christ."[8] The theology is also signified by the rainbow, the token of the covenant, and though not the covenant of grace, yet of kindness and preservation. The rainbow was an emblem of peace and reconciliation by Christ, the Mediator of the covenant of grace, and may assure believers of the everlasting love of God to his people, as well as the immovableness of the covenant of

7   Romans 6:4.
8   1 Peter 3:21.

95

his peace with them.[9]

In the line of Shem, the son of Noah, the knowledge of this kind of theology was continued. Noah's blessing of Shem is thought, by the Cabalists, to contain his earnest desire that he might be the Redeemer of men. However, God was the Lord of Shem, known, owned, and professed by him; and he was the father of all the children of Eber. According to the Jews, Shem had a divinity school where the sons of Japheth, becoming proselytes, dwelt. This school is said to have continued to the times of Isaac, as he is reported to go there to pray for Rebecca. According to them, Eber also had such a divinity school, where Jacob was a minister, servant, or disciple. Continuing these schools, Abraham is said to have one in the land of Canaan, where his three-hundred trained servants are supposed to be his catechumens. He had one also in Haran, where it is said that Abraham taught and proselyted the men, and Sarah the women. However, whatever the case is with these hypothetical divinity schools, this we are sure of, Abraham instructed and commanded his children, and his household after him, to

9   Isaiah 54:9–10.

keep the way of the Lord, and to do justice and judgment.[10]

Moreover, as the gospel was preached to Abraham, there is no doubt but that he preached it to others.[11] Abraham preached according to the knowledge he had of the Messiah, who should spring from him, in whom all nations of the earth would be blessed, and of whom he saw his day and was glad. Founded on this teaching, Abraham's grandson Jacob had a more dear and distinct view of the Messiah, as God's salvation, as the Shiloh, the peacemaker and prosperous one, who should come before civil government was removed from the Jews. And Jacob knew that when Messiah would come, multitudes should be gathered to him.[12]

Idolatry within this period first began among the builders of Babel. Some say it began in the days of Serug, as it was embraced by the Zabians in Chaldea, and obtained in the family of Terah, the father of Abraham. The worship of the sun and moon prevailed in the times of Job, in Arabia, who lived about the time of the children of Israel being in Egypt, and a little before their coming out of it. Yet Job does

10   Genesis 18:19.
11   Galatians 3:8.
12   Genesis 49:10–18.

97

not appear to have given into the idolatry of that people. As for Job and his three friends, it is plain they had great knowledge of God and divine things. They understood by some degree the perfections of God, the impurity of human nature, the insufficiency of man's righteousness to justify him before God, and of the doctrine of redemption and salvation by Christ.[13]

Moses to David

The next period is from the giving of the law to Israel, by the hand of Moses, to the times of David and the prophets. Through this period, supernatural theology was taught by types; these types include the Passover, the manna, the brazen serpent, and other things which were emblems of Christ and his grace, and salvation by him. During this period sacrifices were instituted, particularly the daily sacrifice morning and evening, and the annual sacrifices on the day of atonement, as well as many other. These sacrifices were typical of, and led the faith of men to, the expiation of sins, to be made by the sacrifice of Christ.

13   See Job 14:4; 19:25, 26; 25:4, 5; 33:23, 24.

The whole ceremonial law, all that related to the priests, their garments, and their work and office, had an evangelical signification; it was the Jews' gospel, which led them to Christ, and to an acquaintance with the things of Christ. This law led the Jews to contemplate what to make of Christ, his grace and righteousness, his being necessary to salvation, the evil nature of sin, the insufficiency of men to make atonement for their sin, the need to fulfil all the law, and how to come by a righteousness answerable to all the law. Moses wrote of Christ, of his prophetic, priestly, and kingly offices, either by type or prophecy. The song of Moses in Deuteronomy 32:1–52 and of Hannah in 1 Samuel 2:1–10 very clearly speak of the perfections of God, of his works of providence and grace, and of the Messiah.

According to the Jews, there was a divinity school in the times of Samuel. Naioth in Ramah is interpreted as a house of doctrine, or school of instruction, of which Samuel was president. Here, Samuel stood over the prophets, teaching and instructing them.[14] There were such schools in later times at Bethel, Jericho, and Gilgal. There were schools even

---

14   1 Samuel 19:18–19.

in the times of Elijah and Elisha, where the sons or disciples of the prophets were trained up in the knowledge of divine things.[15] The Targum, in Jerusalem, was a college or house of instruction, where Huldah, the prophetess dwelt.[16] There were within this time some attacks against the true knowledge and worship of God, by the idolatry of the calf at Sinai, of Baalpeor on the borders of Moab, and of Baalim and Ashtaroth and other deities. These pagan intrusions increased after the death of Joshua, and in the times of the Judges.

David to Babylon

The period from the time of David including to the Babylonian captivity abounds with evangelic truths, and doctrines of supernatural theology. The Psalms of David are full of spiritual and evangelical knowledge; many intimations are given of the sufferings and death of Christ, of his burial, resurrection from the dead, ascension to heaven, and session at the right hand of God. So many blessings of grace depend upon what is held within the Psalms, which could never

15   2 Kings 2:3, 5; 4:38.
16   2 Kings 22:14.

have been known but by divine revelation.

The prophets, who follow David, speak out still more clearly for the illumination of those in darkness. They speak of the incarnation of Christ, point out the very place where he was to be born, and the country where he would preach the gospel. They plainly describe him in his person, offices, the sufferings he should undergo, and the circumstances of them, and benefits arising from them. These evangelists bear witness to the doctrines of pardon of sin through him, justification by him, and of his bearing sin and making satisfaction for it.

In short, a scheme of evangelic truths may be deduced from the prophetic writings. Indeed, the great apostle Paul himself said no other things than what the prophets did. Even so, there were some sad revolts from the true God, and his worship, within this compass of time. These revolts are observed in the reigns of some of the kings of Israel and Judah, such as the idolatry of the calves in the reign of Jeroboam, other idolatries by the kings of Israel, and the idolatries committed in the times of Ahaz, Manasseh, and Amon, kings of Judah, which ushered in the captivities of both people.

Babylon to Christ

The period from the Babylonian captivity to the times of Christ finish the Old Testament dispensation. At the return of the Jews from captivity, who brought no idolatrous worship with them, there was a reformation made by Ezra and Nehemiah, with the prophets of their time. Following this reformation, or even during it, the prophets Haggai, Zachariah, and Malachi all prophesied of Christ the Savior, and of the salvation that should come by him. They preach of the several blessings of salvation, speak of the Christ's near approach, point at the time of his coming, and explain the work he should do when come. But after the death of these prophets, and the Holy Spirit departed, there was no more prophecy, and supernatural theology began greatly to decline. During this time, the truths of revelation were neglected and despised, and the doctrines and traditions of men were preferred to the word of God. So it was that the Word took no effect in the spiritual lives of the people.

The sect of the Sadducees, a sort of free-thinking group, rose up and said there was no resurrection, no angels, and no spirit. The sect of the Pharisees, a sort of free-will group, set up traditions as the rule of men's worship, and this group rose to an enormous popularity in the times of Christ, who severely inveighed against them. These are the men of whom their body of traditions were, in later times, compiled and put together in a volume called the Mishnah. This, in course of time, occasioned a large work finished in Babylon and from there called the Babylonian Talmud, which is their doctrinal, or body of doctrine. The Pharisees' collection of writings is full of fables, false glosses, and interpretations of Scriptures; it is the foundation of the erroneous doctrines and practices of the Jews to this day.

George Eliezer Edzard's interpretation

And here I will take leave to transcribe the interpretation of the vision in Zechariah 5:6–11 given by that learned man George Eliezer Edzard (1661–1737)—it being very ingenious and uncommon, and much to our present purpose. This learned man observes from Zechariah that the preceding vision of the flying roll describes the sad corruption of manners among the Jews, in the three or four former ages of the second temple. Though doctrine remained pretty sound among them, their corruption of manners was punished by the incursions of the Lagid Dynasty and Seleucid Dynasty, kings of Egypt and Syria, into Judea, as the vision represents.

Edzard interprets next the following vision of a woman sitting in an ephah, and shut up in it, and then transported by two other women into the land of Shinar. This woman, who, by way of eminency, is called "wickedness," is understood as the impious and false doctrine devised by the Pharisees and Sadducees. Included with her are the other corrupt doctors of the Jews in the latter times of the second temple, and whose teaching would be handed down to posterity. These doctrines are compared to a woman, because they had nothing manly, nothing true, nothing solid in them. Moreover, such theology caused its followers to commit spiritual fornication, as they cannot help but be allured to it by its paints, flatteries, and prittle-prattle. This theology is called wickedness because of all that is defiled by it; not only the tangential fundamentals, but the primary fundamentals, and principal articles of faith—those truths concerning the mystery of the trinity, the deity of the Son of God, and of the Holy Spirit, the person and office of the Messiah. This wickedness not only removes and defiles such truths but puts in their stead false substitutes, traditions, precepts, and inventions of men. This defiling woman brings followers into greater impiety which cannot be thought of; such corruption that would usher in the contempt, rejection, and crucifixion of the Messiah, sent as the Saviour of the world. This defilement would continue in the persecution of the preachers of the gospel, putting a stop to the course of evangelism, as much as it could be stopped, and would draw with it a train of other sins.

The ephah, Edzard thinks, designs the whole body of the people of the Jews, throughout Judea, Samaria, and Galilee. The ephah was first seen as empty, and this being a dry measure, with which wheat and such like things were measured, the food of the body, a proper type of the heavenly doctrine, the food of the soul.[17] By the emptiness of the Ephah is intimated that, around the time of the Messiah's coming, sound doctrine would be banished out of Judea, and the neighboring parts. At this time most of the inhabitants would be destitute of the knowledge of the pure faith. The wicked woman sitting in the midst of the Ephah, and filling it—not just a corner but the whole of it, not lying down but sitting—denotes the total corruption of doctrine, as well as noting the

17   Zechariah 5:6.

wicked woman's power and prevalence throughout Judea, Samaria, and Galilee. She has spread her doctrine, obtaining influence in all places, synagogues, schools, and seats, and pulpits, and among all sorts of inhabitants. Those few remaining in sound doctrine are thus crushed—all who professed the sound doctrine of the trinity, and of the person and office of the Messiah.

And where a "talent of lead" was seen "lifted up," this signifies the divine decree concerning the destruction of the Jews and their polity by the Romans. This Roman lead should be most surely executed on them, for their corruption of doctrine, and for sins that flowed from there. The lifting up of the talent not only prefigured the near approach of the judgment before it was executed but lifting as to set it before the eyes of all the people, to be beheld through the ministry of Christ, and his apostles. Here there is seen hope that, if it might be, some would be brought to repentance, and to acknowledge the true Messiah. The success of this failed, and the talent was "cast into the ephah," and upon the woman in it, signifying the destruction of the Jews. The angel that talked with Zachariah the prophet, was no other than the Son of God, the prophecy's principal author.

Vespasian, and the Roman army under him, are only the ministers and instruments. Even though the talent strikes the woman, the corrupt doctrine was not wholly extinguished, but it was depressed, and weakened, and reduced. The temple and city were burned—that is the chief seat of the defiled doctrine—and the schools throughout Judea destroyed, in which it was propagated. So, a great number of the doctors and disciples were slain or cast into exile, therefore the doctrines were held among only a few.

But in process of time the Jews restored some schools in Palestine, as at Jabneh, Zippore, Caesarea, and Tiberias, in the last of which Rabbi Judah Hakkadosh, also called Judah the Prince (135–*c*.217), compiled the Mishnah around AD 150. After the Mishnah, the next to be published was the Jerusalem Talmud, AD 230. After the death of the Rabbi Judah, his chief disciples went into Babylon, and carried with them the greatest part of the doctors and their scholars out of Palestine. The doctrine little by little disappeared in Judea, and entirely about the year 340, when Rabbi Hillel II (holding office in the Sanhedrin between 320–385) died. He was the last of those promoted doctors in the land of Israel. After this scarce anything was heard of the schools or the wise men of Palestine.

But schools continued in Babylon for many ages; this is what is meant, in the last part of the symbolic vision of Zechariah, by the ephah being carried by two women into the land of Shinar, so called Babylon. By these "two women" are meant the Misnic and Gemaristic doctors; the two heads of these schools were Raf, or Abba Arikha (175–247), and Samuel of Nehardea (c.165–c.254), who went into Babylon a little after the death of Rabbi Judah the Prince, their saint. These two schools carried the woman, false doctrine, along with them. These two are said to have "wings like storks," fit for long journeys, to fly with on high, and with swiftness, into remote parts. This wording fitly describes the above persons transporting their false doctrine into the remote parts of Babylon, far from Palestine, carrying great numbers from that time forward. They did all this without weariness, and with as much celerity as they could. As they made this journey, "the wind" being "in their wings" denotes the cheerfulness with which the Jewish Rabbis pursued their studies until they had finished their design, the Talmud, which they could not perfect without the impulse and help of an evil spirit, signified by this wind. And here in Babylon they "built a house" for their false doctrine, erected various schools, in which it was taught and propagated. And so the doctrine of wickedness was "established" and "set on its own base," and continued for eight hundred and twenty years or more.

This is the sense which this learned man gives of the vision, on which I shall make no more remarks than I have done. Edzard clarifies the source of the corruption of doctrine among the Jews, and shows how it continues, and observes its various means. I will simply state, I think it is ingenious and uncommon, and suits the subject of theology which I have introduced and upon which we continue.

SIX

Pagan theology

Having traced supernatural theology, or divinity, to the times of Christ, let us take a little look back upon the theology of the Pagans before we proceed any further.

The development of Paganism

At, or a little after, the building of Babel, and the dispersion of the people, idolatry began to appear. Knowledge of the true God was greatly lost, and the worship of him neglected. Some say this began in the days of Serug (Gen. 11:20–23), but perhaps it might be earlier. The first objects of it seem to be the sun and moon, which may be deduced quite clearly in the times of Job. Then, it followed the worship of kings and heroes, whom they deified after death, and which at length issued in a multiplicity of gods throughout the several nations of the earth. Whatever truth remained among them was disguised with fables. To use the apostle's phrase, they "changed the truth of God into a lie, and worshipped and served the creature more than the Creator," their foolish hearts being darkened.[1]

The theology of the Pagans, according to themselves, as observed in both Publius Mucius Scaevola (*c.*176 BC–115 BC) and Marcus Terentius Varro (116 BC–27 BC), was of three sorts.

1. Mystic, or Fabulous—which belonged to the poets, and was sung by them.

2. Physic, or Natural—which belonged to the philosophers, and were studied by them.

3. Politic, or Civil—which belonged to princes, priests, and people; being instituted by the one, exercised by the other, and enjoined the people.

Mystic theology

The first of these may well be called fabulous, as treating of

---

1   Romans 1:25.

Hesiod's *Theogony*[2] and genealogy of their deities. In this sort of theology, they say such things as should be unworthy of deity, ascribing to them thefts, murders, adulteries, and all manner of crimes. Therefore, this kind of theology is condemned by the wiser sort of heathens as nugatory and scandalous. The writers of this sort of theology were the Phoenician Sanchuniathon, and of the Grecians, Orpheus, Hesiod, Pherecydes, etc.

Physic theology

The second sort, called physic or natural, was studied and taught by the philosophers. They, rejecting the multiplicity of gods introduced by the poets, brought their theology to a more natural and rational form. They supposed that there was but one supreme God, which they commonly make to be the sun—or at least as an emblem of him. This supreme being is at too great a distance to mind the affairs of the world, and therefore devised certain demons, which they considered as mediators between the supreme God and man. The doctrines of these demons, to which the apostle is

2   A poem from the 8th–7th centuries concerned with explaining the origins and genealogies of the ancient Greek gods and goddesses.

thought to allude in 1 Timothy 4:1, led the philosophers to grow in concern as to studying their nature, office, and with regard to men. Such philosophers who worked in studying these doctrines were Thales, Pythagoras, Plato, and the Stoics.

Civil theology

The third part, called politic or civil, was instituted by legislators, statesmen, and politicians. The first among the Romans was Numa Pompilius (753 BC–673 BC). This theology chiefly respected gods, temples, altars, sacrifices, and rites of worship, all of which properly served their idolatry. The care of all this service belonged to the priests, who then enjoined the service upon the common people, to keep them in obedience to the civil state. Thus, things continued in the Gentile world, until the light of the gospel was sent among them. The times before this light were "times of ignorance,"[3] as the apostle calls them. The Gentiles were ignorant of the true God and the worship of him, of the Messiah and salvation by him. Their state is truly described in Ephesians 2:12,

3   Acts 17:30.

that they were then "separate from Christ, alienated from the commonwealth of Israel and strangers to the covenants of promise, having no hope, and without God in the world." And consequently, their theology was insufficient for their salvation.

SEVEN

The glory of Christ in theology

But we return to supernatural theology and where we left it, having traced it to the times of Christ—at his coming, through his ministry, of his forerunner, and of his apostles—this theology revived and lifted its head. Thus, it appeared in all its purity, splendor, and glory.

The revelation of Christ

John was a man sent from God to bear witness to the light that was just rising, even the Sun of righteousness, the Dayspring from on high. John bore witness of the great Light that should lighten those that sat in darkness with a supernatural light. John declared the kingdom of heaven, or gospel dispensation, was at hand, and was just being ushered in.

He preached the baptism of repentance for the remission of sin, and administered that gospel ordinance. "God, who at various times and in various ways spoke in time past to the fathers by the prophets, has in these last days spoken to us by His Son."[1] Christ his only begotten Son, who lay in his bosom, came and declared of God; who and what he was, and what was his mind and will. Christ brought the doctrines of grace and truth with him, and spoke such words of grace, truth, and wisdom, as never man spoke. His doctrine was not human, but divine; it was not his own as man, he received it from his Father, and delivered it to his apostles. These apostles, having a commission from him to preach, and being qualified for the task with the gifts and graces of his Spirit in great abundance, went into all the world and preached the gospel to every creature. Through this gospel, they diffused the savor of his knowledge in every place. They had the deep things of God revealed to them, things which could never have been discovered by the light of nature nor were revealed in the law of Moses. These apostles received things "eye has not seen, nor ear heard, nor have entered

---

1   Hebrews 1:1–2.

into the heart of man."[2] This is the reason why men could never have understood the gospel otherwise, because the apostles spoke the wisdom of God in a mystery, the hidden wisdom which God ordained before the ages for our glory."[3]

The revelation of the New Testament

In the books of the New Testament are written, as with a sunbeam, those truths of pure revelation, the doctrines of the trinity of divine persons in the Godhead; of the eternal sonship, distinct personality and deity of Christ, and of his several offices as Mediator; and of the distinct personality and deity of the Holy Spirit. These truths speak of God's operations of grace upon the souls of men, of the everlasting and unchangeable love of the three divine persons to the elect, of the predestination of them to the adoption of children, and of their eternal election in Christ to grace and glory. They enlighten upon the covenant of grace made with the elect in Christ and the blessings of it, of redemption by Christ, full pardon of sin through his blood, free justification from sin by his righteousness, and plenary satisfaction

2   1 Corinthians 2:9.
3   1 Corinthians 2:7.

for it by his atoning sacrifice. Such truths speak of regeneration, or the new birth, effectual calling, conversion, and sanctification by the efficacious grace of the Spirit. They tell of the saints' final perseverance in grace to glory, of the resurrection from the dead, and of a future state of immortal life and happiness. All such doctrines are brought to light by the gospel of Christ. These are the sum and substance of supernatural theology, and the glory of it.

And while the apostles continued, and other ministers of the word raised up in their times, these doctrines were held fast and held forth with great clearness and perspicuity. But, as the historian says, after the holy company of the apostles had ended their lives, and that generation was gone—which was worthy to hear the divine wisdom—then a system of impious error took place. Through the deceit of false teachers, false doctrine was attempted to be introduced in opposition to the truth of the gospel, which had been preached. Not one of the apostles was remaining to oppose it.

The doctrines of divine revelation that Satan, by his emissaries, set himself against to undermine and destroy were the doctrines of the trinity, the incarnation of Christ of a virgin, his proper deity, as by some, and his real humanity, as by others. Satan attacked Christ's eternal sonship, or his being begotten of the Father before all worlds. The school at Alexandria, from where came several of the Christian doctors, as Pantaenus (120–216), Clement, Origen, etc. served very much to corrupt the simplicity of the gospel. Though they thought to mend the Platonic philosophy, through it they marred the Christian doctrine. Thus, they laid the foundation for Arianism and Pelagianism, which in later times so greatly disturbed the church of God. As many of the fathers of the Christian church were originally pagans, they were better skilled in demolishing paganism than in building up Christianity, and, indeed, they set themselves more to destroy the one than to illustrate and confirm the other. There was a purity in their lives, but a want of clearness, accuracy, and consistency in their doctrines.

The beginning of Christian heresy

It would be endless to relate how much the Christian doctrine was obscured by the heretics that rose up in the latter part of the first century and on into the second. After this period, we find Sabellians, Photinians, Samosatenians, Arians, Eutychians, Nestorians, Macedonians, Pelagians, etc.

Even still, God was pleased to raise up instruments to stop their progress while preserving the truth, and sometimes very eminent instruments. There is, for instance, Athanasius against the Arians, and Augustine against the Pelagians. The gospel in its simplicity, through the power of divine grace attending it, made its way into the Gentile world, in these first centuries with great success, and paganism decreased before it. And within the times of Constantine, paganism received a fatal blow in the Roman empire. Yet, by degrees, Pagan rites and ceremonies were introduced into the Christian church. And with such rites and ceremonies, errors in doctrine, and other things concurring, made way for the man of sin to appear. That mystery of iniquity, which had been secretly working from the times of the apostles, was finally able to show his head openly. So, at this stage, the man of sin brought in the darkness of popery upon almost all that bore the Christian name.

EIGHT

The reformation of theology

A set of men call the Schoolmen, flourished throughout the twelfth, thirteenth, and fourteenth centuries. These men framed a new sort of divinity called scholastic theology. The first founder of this system is considered by some to be Damascene or John of Damascus (*c.*660–*c.*750), among the Greeks. Others consider the founder to be Lanfranc (*c.*1010–1089), Archbishop of Canterbury, among the Latins. Although generally Peter Lombard (1096–1160) is reckoned the father of these schoolmen. Lombard was followed by our countryman Alexander Hales (*c.*1170 or *c.*1185–1245), and after him were Albertus Magnus (*c.*1200–1280), Bonaventure (*c.*1217–1274), and Thomas Aquinas. Following these men came Duns

Scotus (c.1265/1266–1308), Durandus of Saint-Pourcain (c.1332–1334), and others. These latter schoolmen founded their divinity upon and confirmed it by the philosophy of Aristotle (384 BC–322 BC). But Aristotle's system was not actually understood by them, and was wrongly interpreted to them. They could not read Aristotle in his own language, Greek, so they were beholden to the Arabic interpreters of him, who led them wrong.

Their theology lay in contentious and litigious disputations, in thorny questions and subtle distinctions, and their whole scheme was chiefly directed to support anti-Christian doctrines, and the tenets thereof. By their means, popish darkness was the more increased, and Christian divinity was banished almost out of the world.

The reformers' light

There was only to be found among a few, the Waldenses and Albigenses, the inhabitants of the valleys of Piedmont, and some particular persons and their followers, such as John Wycliffe (c.1328–1384), John Huss (c.1372–1415), and Jerome of Prague (1379–1416). So things continued until the reformation began by Huldrych Zwingli (1484–1531) and Martin Luther (1483–1546), and carried on by others, by whose means evangelical light was spread through many nations in Europe. The doctrines of the apostles were revived, and supernatural theology once more lifted its head. The reformed churches published their confessions of faith, and many eminent men wrote common places, and systems of divinity. In publications they all agreed in the main, to support the doctrines of revelation, of the Trinity and the deity of the divine persons in it, of predestination and eternal election in Christ, of redemption by him, pardon of sin by his blood, and justification by his righteousness.

Always be reforming

But Satan, who envied the increasing light of the gospel, soon began to bestir himself, and to play his old game which he had done with so much success in the first ages of Christianity. He was for a long time otherwise engaged; he continued to nurse up the man of sin, to bring him to the height of his impiety and tyranny, and to support him in it. But his kingdom was likely shaken, if not subverted, by the doctrines of the Reformation. He, as I say, went to his old work again, and revived the Sabellian and Photinian errors;

by the Socinians in Poland and the Pelagian errors, by the Arminians and Remonstrants in Holland. Through this pernicious influence, these doctrines have spread in other countries. They have indeed drawn a veil over the glory of the Reformation, and the doctrines of it.

The doctrines of pure revelation are almost extinguished.[1] Some are endeavoring to bring us, as fast as they can, into a state of paganism, only somewhat refined. It is a day of darkness and gloominess—a day of clouds and of thick darkness—the darkness is growing upon us, and night may be expected.[2] Yet for our relief it is declared, "that at evening time it will be light."[3] Almost all the old heresies are revived under a fond and foolish notion of new light, even when they are no other than what have been confuted over and over. These men please themselves that they are their own inventions when they are the devices of Satan, with which he has deceived men once and again. When men leave the sure word, the only rule of faith and practice, and follow their own fancies and the dictates of their carnal

1   Original: exploded.
2   Joel 2:2.
3   Zechariah 14:7.

minds, they go wrong, and fall into labyrinths, out of which they cannot find their way: "To the law, and to the testimony! If they do not speak according to this word, it is because there is no light in them."[4]

Perseverance

Let us therefore search the Scriptures, to see whether our doctrines are advanced according to them or not. Such a practice, I fear, is too little attended. Upon the whole, as I suggested at the beginning of this writing, I have but little reason to think *A Body of Doctrinal and Practical Divinity* will meet with a favorable reception in general. Yet if it may be a means of preserving sacred truths, of enlightening the minds of any into them, or of establishing them in modern believers, I will not be concerned at what evil treatment I may meet with from the adversaries of these doctrines. Be that as it may, I will have the satisfaction of having done the best I can for the promoting truth, and of bearing a testimony to it.

---

4   Isaiah 8:20.

Discussion Questions

Introduction

1. Why does Gill see it as his duty to clarify doctrine for his congregation?

2. Gill begins his argument for doctrine within his church by stating it is "spiritually understood, affectionately embraced, and powerfully and feelingly experienced." What may be some reasons the church has not associated doctrine with these phrases?

3. How have you understood doctrine to influence good works, or spiritual invigoration?

Chapter 1

1. Why might there be a prejudice against formulating a system of theology compared with other sciences? How would you argue for the necessity of better organizing

a pattern of beliefs?

2. How do Gill's examples from the Bible consistently point toward the cross of Christ help to identify a need for systematizing doctrine?

3. How has systematizing doctrine helped you in your spiritual life? How might the personal practice of organizing articles of faith benefit a richer spiritual life?

Chapter 2

1. What is meant when Gill discusses the "analogy of faith"?

2. What are some weaknesses for using only the bare words of Scripture when formulating theology? What are the benefits, in your own estimation, for working to interpret Scripture by your own words and reason?

3. Gill speaks of different unorthodox (or outright heretical) groups and the language they utilize. What sorts of groups and language are you accustomed to hearing today? How might a better understanding of definitions be useful in helping new Christians guard themselves from heresy?

Chapter 3

1. Though Gill does not intend to "scruple" with the wording, why does he prefer the word *divinity* when referring to the science of God? What other words help us in understanding what we are pursuing in this little book? How would you define theology or divinity to a new Christian?

2. How does Christian theology and doctrine differ from the development of Greek theologies? How does our system of doctrine effect our personal spiritual development differently than ancient Greek religion?

3. What are the most important items to include in a system of theology? Why should a pattern or sequence matter?

Chapter 4

1. Why is it important for Gill to emphasize that God revealed himself prior to the fall? How does our understanding that Adam had a "constant and diligent contemplation of the works of creation" challenge our approach to the science of God?

2. What is the role of natural theology in our personal

spiritual growth? What guidelines should be set forth regarding natural theology to protect a new believer as they seek to know God?

3. Why, following the fall, did God choose to speak of saving knowledge for your benefit?

Chapter 5

1. Why would God desire to build backwards, echoing the cross of Christ, even to the first chapters of his revelation?

2. Based on a system of theology, how were the doctrines of grace made evident through Old Testament history prior to the Gospels?

3. Note the method of interpreting Ezekiel by George Edzard. What are the strengths and weaknesses in this method of understanding the selected passage? How could this method help or hinder your personal study of Scripture? What effects might this interpretation have on a new believer?

Chapter 6

1. How are the developments of pagan theology different

than the progressive revelation of Christian Scripture? Gill has previously noted the truth of doctrine preceding our receiving revelation; how does this challenge a pagan system?

2. What are the key differences between mystic and physic theology? How have these types of religion survived in our communities and churches today?

3. Why do we turn to human law and order (civil theology) when we move away from personal salvation regarding theology? How might justice take different forms between paganism and Christianity?

Chapter 7

1. Gill states that "doctrine was not human, but divine." Why is it vital for Gill and for Christ's church, to emphasize the idea that God revealed his doctrine rather than human beings constructed a system or science on their own?

2. Why would Satan seek to destroy the pursuit of doctrine? Where have you faced temptation or trial in receiving or sharing a systematic formulation of Christian doctrine?

3. How would you see the pagan theologies, the bare words arguments, and the prejudices against systematizing doctrine affecting the spiritual growth and unity of the early church?

Chapter 8

1. Going back to the purpose of Gill's writing this introduction, why does Gill's (and our own) congregation need to recognize the negative response to systematic theology? Why must the congregation be acquainted with words about sound doctrine?

2. What are the main issues facing the church today? What does perseverance through these issues look like?

3. Why does Gill assume he will find an unfavorable reception to his *Body of Doctrinal and Practical Divinity*? What ways can you continue Gill's work in your own church by supporting spiritual growth through doctrine that is "spiritually understood, affectionately embraced, and powerfully and feelingly experienced?"

THE *John Gill* PROJECT

The eminent Baptist pastor-theologian John Gill (1697–1771) is a towering figure in Baptist thought and life. The late D. Martyn Lloyd-Jones thought of Gill as "a man, not only of great importance in his own century, but a man who is still of great importance to all of us." But more than a mere Baptist theologian, the growing retrieval movement of classically Reformed orthodox theology also places Gill among the greatest theologians in the Great Tradition. Therefore, The London Lyceum, The Andrew Fuller Center, and H&E Publishing have partnered together to form the John Gill Project with the mission to republicize the work of John Gill for a new generation of pastors, students, and scholars in dire need of historical resources that remain resolutely committed to classic orthodox Christian doctrine.